The Midnight Horror Tree

The Midnight Horror Tree

Janette Stowell

HEADLAND

First published in 2009
by
HEADLAND PUBLICATIONS
38 York Avenue
West Kirby, Wirral
CH48 3JF

British Library Cataloguing in Publication Data.
A full CIP record for this book is available from the British Library
ISBN: 978 1 902096 53 7

Printed in Great Britain by
Oriel Studios, Orrell Mount
Hawthorne Road
Merseyside L20 6NS

HEADLAND acknowledges the financial
assistance of Arts Council England.

CONTENTS

For Ade

&

Grandad Ernie

Gull

For Stevo

Above the city's horns,
the gull's dirty laughter
shatters noon.

I've heard them say
the gull is a reincarnated fisherman.
I look away
when he warms his ass
on the hot-rocks of town roofs.

A great uncle once rooted feet
on the decks of hatch-battened trawlers –
cheeks birched by driving wind, salt-chewed
eyes, his gloveless palms
guided in the nets.

The gull picks fights
over lunchtime crusts,
but once he feasted on the splintered
wood of a crow's nest – with every list,
his nostrils filled with the ocean's truth.

It's a dicey flight
between birth and death,
though I've yet to see a gull's brains
liquefied on the road's edge
or his wingtips lashing
at the bars in zoos.

He preferred to box his way
down the back streets
of every great port. The one time
he fell, old sea-dogs licked iron
from his wounds.

The gull is above the city.
Surfing the sky's rollers,
he traces slate
to dock.

Years back, he knocked
great slabs of ice
from a herring boat's mast,
knowing the vessel
would soon keel.

The wind is rising.

When the incoming gale
bludgeons the coast,
the gull will continue to fuck
on the edge of a high cliff.

Schizophrenia Antarctica

At first not a catspaw of wind,
just sunlight diffracting
on scalloped ice
and the curved wings
of a distant skua.

Not a pod of sound
roused from rookeries
or a bull seal's harem - nothing
but her isolation

distorting reality and so soon
the frown of dark clouds
gathering suspicion. Listen:

groans beneath pack ice, the stress
of trapped floes and the cracks
beginning to show - tortured fissures
exhaling frost-smoke
with the vertical retch
of a blue whale's breath.

Her anger's depth: gigantic frost blocks
scourged from heart and hurled
beyond crevasses; the convulsions

evoking katabatic winds
that rack glaciers
and the proud tiers of Mount Erebus
dissolving into whiteout.

Fifty-Four Degrees South

Beyond forty degrees south, there is no law; beyond fifty degrees
south, there is no God – old whalers saying

I wrote this poem on Grytviken beach,
then settled on a high rock to simply watch.
A penguin scuffed the crude ruck of night.
A seal dragged its weight from innard to sweat.
The waves skulked in to sniff my last line,
skulked out again.
A southwesterly rain
turned the rest to slush.

*

But nothing could stop the whalers.
Below the processing factories, the beach
was buried under sturdy flensing plans –
enormous chopping blocks
on which the warm mammals
were decapitated, sawn open, dismembered,
gutted. Oily blood and innard gunk
roiled down wooden decks
and for months on end Grytviken's waters were red:
miles of sea clagged with bones and blubber
and the hull-fucked ships
had no need to drop anchor. Raving night
tethered to the black smoke
that fumed from cookeries
and coagulated with the stench
of festering meat and sweat
because everyone stank,
even the priest.

Back then, no waves
skulked in or out
and the penguins, the seals, the poets
kept well away.

Storm Force

I. EXT. IRISH SEA. NIGHT

Mid-winter. Scathing
south-easterly gale. The exorcism
of colossal waves and a ship
lurching from swell.
An almighty thud: violent
punch to the ferry's hull.

Blackout.

Fade in to: ampoules of colour - the lights
            from a distant rig.

II. INT. SHIP'S SALON. NIGHT

A dog whines. Passengers hunch
over knees. Last suppers
crump into sick-bags. Malefic creaks
from metal frames
and the pitted floors -
a momentary suspension
before the ship
rears up.

Behind closed hatches
crockery crashes -
the great ninth wave
rabid on portholes,
the force nine gale
fist-fucking the funnels.

V.O. The grey wolf waits
        in the halls of the gods.

III. EXT. SEABED. NIGHT

Silence
as a lone crab
balances the ocean
on its latticed back.

Crabs

I

Having no idea
how to cook crustaceans,
mum set four live crabs
in a pan of cold water, turned on the hob.
She was vacuuming the front room
when the water started to boil,
did not hear the low reedy whistles
that skewered the kitchen's steam.

Then suddenly, and even over
the high drone of hoover,
she heard the acute
cacodemonic squeals
of death by heat.

II

Once, the crabs crept across floors
slackened by sulfide rubble, down
to the old mills of aquatic landscapes.
The black smokers had unusual features:
tall, warped, heat-heckled flues - their vent shafts
hotter than three hundred degrees -
from which the crabs fled, preferring
cooler strolls to coral beds.

III

There was a sign
above the door: *Welcome
to Punta Arenas – a City at the End
of the World*. Keen for any
Armageddonic view, she took
a window seat and ordered
the day's dish.

The table wobbled
as the waiter settled
the platter. The crab's meat
was served in its own
huge orange carapace: a dead sun
with stiff rays kicking
pitted wood.

The Midnight Horror Tree

Dusk flagging on Mount Kinabalu,
seeping through rock
and the curve of a valley
stretched to jungle
where daylight is lost.

Dusk slumped in stony gutters
and the long arid road
where shady creped faces
sell parrots and orchids.

But now, with the slick of night en route,
a foul scent coils from the Midnight Horror -
dense ammonia
swamping a hot breeze
that seethes in distant shacks.

And soon the sky will throb: a louring mass
of bats, nostrils enflamed
as they clamp claws onto putrid, bulbous corollas
to breathe in life.

Then later, when dinting back to cool caves,
they will bring blue funks to a thatch-maker
who leans on his porch - a shadow
lengthening under the mangrove tree
where, each night, fireflies settle
and breathe out light.

The Midnight Horror Tree (Oroxylum Indicum) is one of six trees
worldwide that is pollinated by bats.

Tramp

Paris. Early morning. The sun
lodged in the city's neck, the streets
quiet and the boulangeries still
closed.

In *Pont Neuf* shadow
a tramp strips, then jumps
into the Seine. Insane
with sleep's drought, he doggy-paddles
from one side of the river, and back.

Afterwards, he stands naked,
his bread-and-dripping limbs
wetting the concrete path. He dresses,
moves on and, before too long,
the patch is dry – gone – almost as if
he had never been there at all.

The Shrieking Sixties

A penguin has escaped
from the city zoo: black claws
on grey stone, orange beak
pointing south, he waddles
into town.

*

Jacked-up on Merrydown,
the man with no home
is reminded of his childhood hero: a survivor
of the Circumpolar Current,

whose lifeboat was tameless
in twenty foot waves,
as the Shrieking Sixties
(those fast, cracked hussies)
mauled ass, hope, sanity,
soul, while the gangrene

munched from toe to dick -
and he got down
on all fours
to bail out the ocean
with his one good boot,

the whole time nothing
but dirty finger nails
and a stray gentoo
for nourishment.

*

On his square of cold pavement,
the man sits upright
and clacks his tongue:

here, Penguin.

River

I come with no rudder
to shatter your ice – no long oars
to scratch shallows
where water-lice suckle
on the flash of metallic spoke and all that

rubber. River, your head's choked
with a city's forgotten journeys: car rides
to parties, seasides, offices,
morgues, and your mind

is stone-weighted skirts and sacks
heavy with infant dogs – the dead strips of bark
that have fallen to roughen
your fugues.

The sleepless have fed you
their thick foamy pads, stained
with the syrups of birth, death
and the crazed killings
of time inbetween

your banks: the hardcrocks
of frozen mudbone
where sprites loiter
and whisper fishy parables
to reeds.

River, you cannot go on
like this.

Bring back the ducks and the quacks
in long coats and latex boots – sleek
rods rousing the larvae
that have slept in your stamens
all winter.

Bring back the soft deck of long grass,
leaf, flower and moss. Let river
boats tug away
your hypothermic
coma.

Scenes from the Hotel Barge

After spring refit, the passengers came.
Still half-drunk from the nights before, we drove them
to wineries, beaches, churches,
and a palaeontology museum
with dinosaur turds in a long glass case,

while the barge mulled its way
up and down canal – through pounds,
locks, tunnels, bridges,

and at each mooring spot a duck
would be gang-raped
under the gangplank.

Sometimes, in the clamp of high summer,
passengers didn't come
and then we drank for twelve hours straight
and fought,

but there's a certain peace
in a thrown glass - a delicate bird
coming to know its flight - though I guess
we'll never sprawl again

on sun-loungers, watching dawn crawl
out from the oyster beds, bleeding a route
to the steep rock of Sète
on the other side of the lake.

This was also the year
when twenty tonnes of fish
rose to the canal's surface – a Chinese burn
on each lung, breath twisted
by toxic waste that turned
the water's edge
a yellow green.

Other times it rained
and the *Tramontane* would run in
with its big mood on,
and we'd hole-up in the wheelhouse
with an oil-lamp and mosquitoes.

They'd chew anywhere:
eyes, waist, bum and the itch
like no other, the centre hotter
than a meteorite's – that flaming oddball
scudding through Midi night.

A red flash of space stone,
and the summer was over.

Wavelengths

It is night. Further down the street,
someone is having a party. Music
overwhelms my room. I fear the walls
will topple, like flimsy beach-huts
hit by cranky waves.

*

In another ocean, a whale snouts
an elegant path through deep waters.
Its melodic grunt rolls
through the peaks and troughs of kilohertz
until its voice is heard by another mammal
fifty miles away.

*

Grandad was a radio ham. He stuck
a ten-foot antenna through the roof,
then spent whole nights on short wave
ragchewing with creatures
on distant continents.

*

Their music gets louder; my threats go unheard.
I hang out the window. Overhead, a star pulses
angry blue, its curses
radiating - intense short wavelengths.
I tune in, listen
to the sharp lisp of light,
then nose my way
back to bed.

Code

A man was snatched from the roadside
by four men in a black car.

Blindfolded and gagged, he was driven
through city streets. There were sounds
beyond his captors' breathing: the buses'
knackered hydraulics, the gloat of sirens,
cathedral bells.

*

Pulled from the car, he was marched
over concrete, then up steep
Piranesian staircases. Eventually, his blindfold
and gag were removed and he was asked,
Where are you?

I am here, he thought, then looked around the room:
no furniture, no windows, walls painted brown,
scruffy floorboards. One scientist
had a gold watch and a front tooth to match.

I'm in the vault of a bank, he said.

*

He is home now, sitting in his garden,
smoking. Above the elm, the sky
is an open atlas, revealing
the chartered nooks of far-flung galaxies.

He thinks back to the brown room – a back room
of an opera house (as it turned out to be).

When released, he had caught
the opening notes of the *Dies Irae*
and the scientists' whispers:

...in conclusion, it's impossible
to comprehend place until the external
has been viewed in its entirety

universe could be packed
into a tree's trunk

latter's markings are certainly similar
to a planet's concentric rings, of course
just a hunch, but still

what do you fancy for lunch?...

His stomach rumbles; the sound
is reassuring. He grinds his cigarette butt
into an old wormhole. At least, he hopes
it's old. Too late now. Drilling starts up
in the neighbourhood: electric work-tools,
or a woodpecker's illiterate Morse.

Smarties

For Margaret

Another Sunday. A stray dog sniffs
its own piss. Even the crows
are bored.

Over the road, three boys
have climbed the bus-shelter
to welly stones at passing cars
and cats.

Me and Marg have done
the slide, the frame, the swing
and are now sprawled on the broken slats
of roundabout. I'm counting out
the Smarties:

> *one for you*
> *one for me*
> *one for you*
> *one for me*
> *one for –*

From above, a fag-furred voice:

> *Frig's sake, you'd think she'd never seen*
> *a fucking Smartie before.*

It's not God, but an older girl
with tantrum-thrower arms
and hair so greasy
it could batter conger-eels.

Our Smarties got left behind. Later,
I imagined the light bag of death
and the disappointment
when the crows discovered the brightly coloured shells
housed no sexy bugs.

Hop Tu Naa

The turnip was carved
into a pentagonal fright:
eyes, nose, mouth and its skull
crammed with pocket torch,
the weak light a nod
to dimming souls
trapped in the stinkhorned dome
of Purgatory.

This was the winter knock-knock:
us kids in swing
to October song -

> *hop tu naa*
> *me mother's gone away*
> *and she won't be back*
> *until the mor-ning...*

- an audience of one, yawning
from a half-open door, as two coins
jangled in the glassy pits
of a Horlicks jar.

Hop Tu Naa (pronounced Hop Tu Nay): a Manx song traditionally sung
from house to house on the night of 31st October

Impressing Daddy

Sunday. Slavonia. Baba Yaga
preparing for flight: blasphemous chants,
a violent shudder, then holding breath
and a new green hat while speeding backwards
down the garden path with the whole world
in reverse. Fast: O²H in a huge iron kettle
           then swoo
shup over the apple tree in a hiss
of wind and the roadside dust and af
        uck
she's forgotten her goggles as church slates
avalanche into tomorrow and God's teeth
how the kettle boggles: turbulation
above (already) the Transylvanian Alps
   so cold   brass balls   and crack
pots galore   then gone
with snow geese and Romanian plains,
navigating a route by gypsy
remains as the compass is useless so: ash pats,
chicken bones and grieving guitars all the way
to the scree-pits that clot Bila Tserkva,
then trailing gaunt maples
to Chemikua where descent begins:
             braking
a heart for an emergency st
op and refuel
at Lake Ladoga
and a swift Scotch egg
in the cafeteria
then shudderswoosh O²H roadside dust and af
        uck
       over Ust'llimstk
when applying new lipstick
and looking out for Daddy
      (who lives now in exile
      on the Siberian plateau)
no doubt half-frozen and certainly longing for af
reakishly good cup of tea.

---

*Baba Yaga: a female demon of Slavonic tradition who flew about in an iron
kettle*

Cot Death

I

New mum plays dead, just listens to the blood
weave through her ears. The doctor inspects
the torn vagina, his tongue
rimming his lips as he threads suture
through the needle's
slit.

II

It's a long room in a Parisian fashion house.
Well-lit. Flowered-up. Posh.
Under the Matisse, a silver trolley
is laden with coffee and cake.
On a marble desk, a telephone
rings, but The Fates will not answer
to anyone.

Clotho pads the spindle's peddle, unravels
the silver thread of life. Lachesis stretches
her tape measure, marks up the length:
one quarter inch. Atropos sighs,
then opens the legs of her golden scissors
and snips.

III

How could you not see your own thread, baby?
It is bioluminescent, radiant, your soul's
bling. Did Daddy not tell you this cord connects
your dream body to your belly?
You may journey outside, if you get my drift,
but roam too far and your thread
will snap.

Great yogis are trained in astral travel.
You, baby, are not.

Mandrake

She couldn't sleep
and twelve doctors
couldn't help.

Her brainpan was scorched black;
blowflies schemed at its edge.

A shaman sold her wine,
full-bodied and pressed
from the Little Gallow Man,

a plant he'd poached from Government ground -
the foot-scuffed tract beneath the noose.

She drank up
and slept for three days,
her heartbeat so deep

it became undetectable.
Then she rose again
and prepared a fish supper

for twelve doctors
and five thousand baby blowfly.

Stop

I

The snow falls black
in Norilsk. Outside the nickel factory,
hard ice winces, then steams. A teacup snaps
in two. Daddy gobs on his daughter's foot
and wails for the firing squad. But no –
she will not fetch him vodka
or pear schnapps. She is not his enabler,
and anyway, Daddy, you said
you would stop.

II

It rarely snows in Douglas. But that day
the rooftops were white, the school rooms
cold, the science teacher adamant:

if a steam train flies down tracks in one direction,
and a bluebottle flies through air in the opposite
direction, when they meet the bluebottle will,
for the minutest fraction of time, stop
the train.

I did not believe this.

III

Summer came, as did the faceless
mascots of totalitarian power - their caterpillar tracks
snuffing cherry blossom and laughter
on Changon Avenue. Striding
into the center of the road, a slim
nineteen-year-old man
rooted his feet and raised his left hand.
His right hand gripped
a bag of groceries – the suggestion of a chore
complete, a quiet stroll home, plans
for dinner.

Heat squalled from rubber tracks
and the veins in the young man's hand
bulged
(like the underground telephone wire
that was swelling with code)
as the forty ton battle tanks
slowed
to a stop.

Ghost Rain

A thirsty cypress, you stand alone
in the rut of Saharan heat
watching rogue cloud
drift through desert sky.

The cumuli is fat
with hardcore tonics. You stretch
your branches wide, bark itching
as wolf spiders scram
down the rigours of trunk.

For the first time in years, you relax
in the soffit of cloud shade, the lush density
of its moisturized zone – the rain
so close, only a few feet
from your highest branch

when it hits hot air
and evaporates.

Cypridina

Go down to Tateyama,
where moon-ridden water
laps at the foot
of an old wooden jetty.

Loop twine
around the head
of a week-dead fish, lower
through tide,
down to the sandy bed.

Wait.

Consider, perhaps, the long nights
of warfare in Iwo Jima: a volcanic island
mean on tree, grass, shelter, cover
for innumerable soldiers lost
in the overlapping fumes of mortar,
and a thousand last breaths.

Too dark, too dangerous
to fire up a match to smoke
or scan a chart, the reason why
Japanese officers kept cigar cases packed

with the gritty dried husks
of luminescent crustaceans: a pinch
in the hand mixed with spit
until the cupped palm glowed
and maps could be read.

Now raise the line, pull in
the bait:

the fish head is preened
with the effulgent bulbs
of cypridina.

A tiny crustacean of the order Ostracoda, cypridina live in the shallow seas of Japan. Even when dead, their luminous fluid can be activated to give off light.

Warhead

The parachute flares lose height
and your metropolis is illuminated
with a turquoise glow. It films
walls and pavement
with exotic shadow.

You smell gas, cordite, rubber,
pepper. The docks have been hit
again and soon the sewers
will back-up – waterlogged turds and bloated rats
pestering sandbags in the doorways
of civic buildings.

You love it. The way dogs and litter levitate
as bombs fall in nearby lanes. How vapour trails
hitch the sky, and leaden waves
kick cats onto high walls. The air's rip
and brilliant flash, as though the moon
had just flung itself into the street.

You love how the porch belches you out.
You skid down steps, cobbles, gutter,
road - the brick dust gritty
like your grandad's liver salts.

You've swallowed teeth. The sweet one croons
in your stomach's depth
and you can do nothing but laugh.

The Poppy Chain

I. AFGHANISTAN

Follow the farmer's back
down mountain path, the dry ruck
of stone, earth, brown.

No sound but the pad
of his bare feet, sun-cooked
and chapped - two wizened professors
in their knowledge of soils.

The night before he scored the pods, slitting
each green bulb
with three sets of four tines
to free the milky juice,
and now the poppies are ready.

The farmer scrapes each flower's cheek
until his spatula is heavy
with the stringy brains of opium gum.
He knocks this pulp to canister
and then, as though his mother
had just made the Sunday bowl of *firni,* he licks
the spoon clean.

II. ENGLISH HOSPICE

Alice is a withered head on hardened pillows.
The tumour in her chest is the size
of a fruit she never liked: too bitter
the one time she tried it. The doctor says,
it's time for her injection.

Alice can see things - scenes from the past
looping from the dark reels of her pupils:

she is running from gurney to gurney, so many
wounds gnashing the nightshift's minutes
as she thrusts hypodermic needles
into necks, arms, buttocks, feet,
and when a man has no
neck, arms, buttocks, feet,
her needle probes beneath loose flaps
of skin, tendon, muscle, nerve,
sometimes touching
bone

and Alice would love that man then,
press a pillow to his cheeks,
sing a romantic anthem
very quietly.

III. ENGLISH CITY CENTRE

Eve walks to work,
through the warm pastry smells
that drift from a bakery door, past
the newsagent's sandwich-board

Local Granny Deals Heroin

then on down Bellside Road
where it starts to rain.
She buys a poppy from an old man
who lets her rap his wooden leg.
Can't feel a thing, he says.

Eve pins red to her coat's black
then ups the pace because she's already
late and on the sky's horizon,
there is nothing
but the grey blot of long haul.

IV. THE CHIPPY

Eve shovels chips into plastic trays
adds sausage, beans, gravy,
then wraps the workman's dinner
in thick paper. Her eyes weep
grease. Her arms are blistered
from the hot spit of fat; then she's wanted
out back:

two large barrels
of onions to peel, floors
to be brushed and mopped, cod
to be fried, bins to be emptied, industrial vats
to be scrubbed, as well as the hot plates
and grill pans with their dark leprous
landscapes.

The sink is deep and nine pots in
Eve's spine is a hellbent
question mark:

Why isn't there a memorial day
for all those lives wasted
in crap jobs?

Then there's a queue out front
and Eve's back
to shoveling chips.

V. AFGHANISTAN

When the farmer awakes,
the sun is burrowing deep
into Hindu Kush soils.
He peels petals
from his neck, arms, buttocks,
feet.

Uncle John

Every fortnight when I went to sign on
I'd meet Uncle John
in the dole queue.

The queue was always as long
as Uncle John's hair and he'd say,
I wish they'd fucking hurry up,
I've got to be back at work
in ten minutes.

Then Uncle John got cancer
and he had to go
to Clatterbridge – so

he borrowed a suit and spent
the price of five pints
on a haircut and looked well
smart.

He was gone for a while and came back
bald and we laughed
when he said he'd been a daft sod
going to that bloody hairdressers.

Uncle John died
and I got a job
because there was no fun anymore
in signing on.

Hamster

Since I got Hamster
I do not spray air freshener
in the bedsit.

Hamster likes grapes and unsalted
nuts but too much trifle
and his little gut curdles.

His cage has three wheels
and a cabbage patch
doll, but he would much rather hang

from laddered lace nets
or the hem of the Argos throw.
Too often I catch him

skating across the radiator top
or along the clammy sill – his nose tip
knotted in concentration.

Our window is always locked
tight. I do not want to see his head
clamped in sharp pincers – the gull's

stern umlaut eyes
and outstretched wing, its acidic mess
spunked on the just-cleaned glass.

I suppose Hamster would love it, the ride.
Sometimes I put him in a wicker basket
and gently swing him from side
to side. I swear
he laughs.

I keep the toilet lid down.

Kettle locked up.
Wires wound.
And the food mixer
is strictly for show.

I just do not know
how people with children
cope.

After the Pub

Down in the kitchen, the chip fat spits.
The cat-flap opens outward, closes shut.
Heat sucks moisture from the dishcloth.

You've fallen asleep on the toilet again.
Your head is lolling above your thighs.

Lard overflows.
The smoke alarm fits.
Bills curl up on the corkboard.

Hairs in your nostrils twitch.
The cactus is now an Olympic torch.

Floorboards cackle.
A wardrobe retches.

Out in the street, Moggy watches
black smoke fleeing an open window.

Your poltergeist's applause
brings down the house.

God's Mug

It used to have a handle
but now two stumps protrude
like spores on a potato.

I LOVE BLACKPOOL

Inside always, a black pool
of cold tea beneath smooth
arboreal rings
that no abrasive pad
will ever remove.

Beyond Full Beam

I was given last rites. By rights,
I should be dead and yet, I am no longer
nil-by-mouth and the deviant
itch of brace on back is a good sign.

There are flowers on the bedside table.
I put a daffodil head to my ear
and a woman says, *Operator,*
how can I help you? in a voice so sweet
it could have slipped from a piping bag.
I try to answer, but instead gargle
loose chippings.

Beyond the window, there's the dull
roll of traffic on city streets.

Recurring montages craze
my white cast: a sharp corner
soused in full beam, the confusion
of brakes, metal, wheels,
and the fox's eyes - citrine quartz
on the roadside bank.

I watched myself being cut
from the prang, my forehead studded with glass
like the top of a neighbour's wall. Then I became
the bloodwagon's light, whirring blue
as the wind shifted
up a gear...

...blue tarmac, blue glass, blue chaos and fox
lapping blue marrow from chevron.

Seurre Noir

I

A one-hearse town. High-tide
mauling a cobbled-stone quay,
the bollards crouched low
under plane trees.

Crumbling streets,
and the pavements grouted
in grime, grit, hardened dogshit.
A café-tabac. The half-clang
from a church bell
as the rain hatches at last.

II

The old café, fucked
a hundred years ago, but still
the Madonna to silent men
who slouch over round tables,
reading damp scriptures
in the rot of woodchip
and Gauloise fug.

The oak door whinges
as a girl steps in from the rain:
a worn-out storm-shaker
in search of a large *pastis*.

III

Ingesting a mouthful of musky air,
the blind man rolls
a magazine - the baton of advertisement
swiped at flies
and the half-dead moth
lost in the folds of his crotch.

The blind man orders the beebread
that has just stepped in from the rain.
Will wash it down with a rare
cognac.

His bill settled, he leaves alone
only the dog-black night
to guide him home.

On Serge Gainsbourg's Grave

A torn yellow garter

      hung

from frozen begonia

empty wine bottle

      and booklet of rain

soaked matches - long-stemmed

         white roses

feathered tits and stained plaque:

      The White & Black Blues

a stack of metro tickets

(weighted with pebbles)

      four sugarcubes beside

a monochrome photograph:

      Young Serge Smoking Gitane

      the dirty cuddly monkey

pinecone and a lipstick tube

         Exces de Rouge, Exces de Rouge

crocus and circus pamphlet

a note on card:

Serge, on t'aime

one raddled brain

of shrunken cabbage – a tribute to

L'Homme À Tête De Chou

lost puddles

in tea-light holders

two fresh lemons

the live jolt

of raucous song and humping

late October air

the hot scent

of *someone's* nuts

roasting

on an ancient griddle.

(Montparnasse Cemetery, October 31st, 2004)

je suis

yellow paint
whirling brush hair I breathe out
bar freight or the smell of fuck
how those bushes shake and smile
blackbird your beak so perfect for stabbing

friends with long tusks
stampeding down church aisles and the gargoyles
watching always watching so loud
so loud the butterfly sucking
fat sap from Oleander
lost deep in the purple caves
of my equator

always always I will eat

the easel dregs tongue sweeping
her thighs her thighs and the black grass
haunts my breath I wash my thumbs
in ruby juice then tip
my orange head and the countryside falls
to knees with wax and stamps
and money orders and wicker
legs I have not known

or dared to run
through dark blue flame I sway
then judge each rigid arm I've thrown
at white scapes the deep throats
of lurid stars and yellowing paint
whirls in hair and ear and wind the wind
getting near getting near

can smell the sunflowers
yellow fear

Love Before Breakfast

I split New York when it started,
jumped trains through twenty states
of paranoia: the twitchy walk
through overnight sleeper, ears cocked
for a whistle, the train dispatcher,
laughter.

I walk the last twenty miles
or so - a desolate and flyblown shuffle
across the flogged bladder
of a dried-up river, then on
through the abandoned lots
of mine, farm, mill. The gas-pumps
at Buttermilk Junction are empty
but a billboard tells me:

There's No Way Like The American Way.

No way I'm poaching
the last Chero from a roadside camp,
the migrant workers wheezing sleep,
faces stuck to sheets
torn from *The Columbus Citizen*:

Kill Ohio Relief Plan, Go Home.

But it's no home: a long-faced rat-coop
knocked up from old pallets, dung, rope,
spit

and no-one in. I holler
Mama? then figure
they'll be working the field, plucking slugs
off the share-cropper's lettuce.

I take it slow down gimcracked streets:
the soda stall's dusty; a sleeping dog
looks tasty; the whore-house porch, thirsty.

But I sit on it anyway, holler
Mama? again.

A kid comes near, puts a blue's harp
to his lips then sucks
twenty states of misery
through his vibrating reeds. Sweet,
but I haven't a cent.

Across town,
the movie-theatre's boarded up
but stuck to the door,
the last lobby card:

Love Before Breakfast

I split New York when it started.

Looking Around

After Neruda

It happens that I'm tired of writing.
It happens that I go into supermarkets,
frisking fruit or cooking chocolate
and the inkwells of yoghurt pots
navigated by metaphor and simile,
I should not go into chemists.

There are bookshops that disgust me:
the repose of soft-backs on sofas,
bookseller recommends, three-for-two trends.
I want to see no more of it.

It happens that I am tired of my pen tip
stuck to the closed buds of my fingers,
and the half moons of my nails
shedding no light.

I do not want to go on
staring through windows and receiving envelopes
that I once addressed to myself. I am tired
of small notebooks and the stolen snippets
of condensation that will rust my journal's lock.

And yet, it would be delicious
to scare an ex-fiancé when winning the Booker
or knock a critic dead with a particularly strong sonnet.
It would be beautiful
to straighten out my compacted spine
and, just once, to write *The End* and mean it.

Janette Stowell was born and raised on the Isle of Man. She currently lives in Liverpool where she teaches Creative Writing at John Moores University and Liverpool University. Poems in this collection have previously been published in the magazines *Mslexia, Back to the Machine Gun, Roundyhouse, In the Red*, and in the books *Poetry Pool: Poems from Liverpool John Moores University* (Headland) and *This Island Now – An Anthology of Manx Poets*.

I am amused by my muse
Too often, sadly, others leave me confused
I ponder, maunder e wearily wonder
I question the theme, fly off in a dream
Other minds plunder 'til names torn
asunder
Resigned, I turn the page.

Fleeting shadows though my shutter,